Broken 2 Redeemed

Amber Talley

Presentation by *BookLeaf Publishing*

Web: www.bookleafpub.com

E-mail: info@bookleafpub.com

ISBN: 9789357441964

First edition 2023

*In Memory of Noah Gray Talley who was
just simply too beautiful for earth.*

Saved As A Little Girl

When I was just a little girl careless and free
I accepted Salvation to secure my eternity.
My daddy prayed with me and helped me with
accepting my own sins
The next week or so I was baptized and my new
life in Christ would begin.
I was different than all the ones at school,
there was times when others around me were so
cruel.
I was made fun of for being so nice and kind
I didn't have too many friends but I really didn't
even mind.
I loved serving within the church and raising
many funds,
for events and places I couldn't attend yet
because I was much too young.
I stayed in church & served from that day on
I thank God for godly parents so that I could still
be in love with Jesus, even when I am grown.

Yes, Broken Crayons Can Color Too

Yes, Broken Crayons Still Can Color

Have you ever been so beat down,
so broken with a loss of everything
feeling so hopeless,

Lost all the desire to know who you are
The pain still remains, like an open scar

They say the window to the world is your soul,
But the sin you are entangled in makes your
heart grow so cold

You cry & cry out with everything you have but
you lose your breath,
Screaming in hopes someone can hear you but
so do demons of death,

You have gone through days of torment and days
of sorrow and pain,
You cry and cry and tear drops fall like the rain

When you finally get sick and tired of feeling so
down,

You must admit to God you are a sinner & in
Christ be found,

Yes, you may be broken but you are able to be
repaired,
Because the Savior of the world died on a cross
so that your life could be spared

I am not the same I was in the past, but it shaped
and molded me,
Now I live for Christ and give Him all the
everlasting glory.

I now spend my days giving thanks to God
above
For His grace, mercy, and His unconditional
love.

It amazes me that Jesus died for a wretched
sinner like me,
But He died to save the sins of everyone for all
eternity.

We are broken crayons but we can still color just
the same,
Giving our lives to Christ, who is the powerful
name above all other names.

Angels Watching our Sorrow

If you have ever loss someone so precious and
so truly dear to you
The days following may come with all sorts of
emotions & pain just out of the blue,

We have peace when we know our loved ones
are saved,
You better make that decision soon as Jesus is
the only way,

We know we have angels watching us from
Heaven so intently
Disguised as miracle occurrences & moments of
complete protecting

Some angels send signs for us to see
Like a feather, butterfly, cardinal or even a
random penny

We will spend our time looking for them in the
most mundane things
After a storm comes a clear sky with clouds that
look like wings

After the rain comes a glorious rainbow

Symbolizing God's true promise the reason we
have hope.

Our loved ones are not suffering anymore with
no more sickness and no more hurting
We long to hug them one more time and talk to
them for hours about our days and all they are
missing.

They are safe from this cruel wicked world and
worshiping beside Jesus everyday
I can imagine they are sitting at grand feast
listening to stories and what He has to say.

So send us butterfly kisses, red cardinals &
dragon flies flying around
For one day soon when we get to Heaven our
loved ones will be at last found.

Noah & The Perfect Promise

If you ever went to Sunday School you were told
the story of Noah a great Godly man,
You see he was told to build this mighty vast ark
for all the rain to withstand.

He did as God told with no hesitation as he
showed his great faith,
He built an ark to keep himself, animals and his
family extra safe.

God instructed him to bring the animals inside
two by two,
With so many animals among his family they
probably didn't know what to do.

It rained for a very very long time
God flooded the earth due to all the sin in the
land and all of the crimes.

The ark provided shelter from the cold wet days
and nights,
It finally stopped raining after countless days
can you imagine what a sight.

God was pleased with Noah's obedience in doing
what he was told,
By this time God sent a glorious rainbow for
him to behold.

He said this was to symbolize a beautiful
promise to never flood the earth again
Somehow this symbol gets twisted into people's
own sins.

We can all learn a lot from Noah with just
listening to what God has to say,
Just stepping out and being obedient in what He
is asking us to do as He will always make a way.

He is a great example of what having faith can
bring
Being more in tuned with God is such a
beautiful thing.

So maybe God is telling you to go out and do
something new,
Something scary, unfamiliar, but know that He
will be right there with you.

The ark was there way of escaping the storm
with no harm to anyone or anything inside the
ark,

When he obeyed, God had protected them from
the cold mornings and evenings so dim and dark

So if God says build you just say "yes, Lord
please give me the proper tools,"
The people that Noah told about the ark looked
at him like he was a complete fool.

I want a pure faith like Noah one so free to do
anything
A faith that is shaped and molded by God with
studying about Him alone daily.

Thank you God for giving us the perfect promise
that you won't flood the world again,
When we see a rainbow next time remember the
story of Noah and God who always wins.

I Love "Those People!"

You see people everywhere you go,
walking around aimlessly going to and fro.
In a world where ones are addicted to alcohol &
drugs,
There are hurting families out there having to
show tough love.
What works for one in recovery isn't the same
for everyone,
Some have rehab, meetings of all kinds, some
have to lose everything to finally be done.
We can argue all day if it's a choice or if it's a
disease
Anything that takes over the mind out of one's
control is both so let's just stop fighting please.
Addiction doesn't discriminate and can happen
to even the very best ones,
Don't think it can't happen because it can occur
to anyone and the addiction has already
overtaken and won.
It comes in many types and many treacherous
forms,
Leaving ones struggling, families broken and
sinning becomes the new norm.
Society looks down on "those people," and gives
condemnation and shame,

I see them as Christ sees them and I know He
can restore and they can change.
"Those people" are my family, friends and all
around me
Don't get too prideful because it can happen to
someone you love without any warning
I love ones in recovery as it's my passion to see
new lives being redeemed,
The ones living just for today and chasing plans
and living out their dreams
Recovery is possible each and everyday
With Christ guiding because He alone is the only
way.
So next time you see "those people" on the street
Be thankful they are here another day as many
before them passed suddenly
Addiction is a sin problem and can hurt loved
ones and others very much so,
Showing tough love isn't always fair or right but
always praying for them is the way to go.
If you are in recovery I am proud of you today
If it's only been a minute, you're a rockstar I'd
gladly say.
I hope you know Jesus before it's much too late,
Make sure that you are ready for Heaven with
that last breath you take.
God gives us multiple chances but we do not
give them usually

Why can't we love one another as we are called
to do and just love unconditionally.
Our world will be a kinder place when families
and friends are mended back together
When addiction doesn't exist anymore and pasts
aren't brought up then love won't be severed.

He Provides

Has there ever been a time when God didn't
come through
When there were things needing fixing, bills
were piling up and there was no food
He is a loving Heavenly Father who always will
provide
His timing may not be what we want but He
asks us to be in His presence & to abide.
He answers our requests that we have made
known unto His ears
Sometimes He doesn't just take away the
problem but gives you peace and gets rid of fear.
He is always an on time God, even when we
don't think He is quick enough
A God who doesn't let us handle anything on
our own and doesn't just leave us stuck.
His promises are always faithful and are amen
and yes
We tend to worry about everything without
giving Him the chance to give us His very best
Our blessings come from all around and
sometimes we are even unaware,
How something is needed and He will send
someone at just the right moment and the
request will be there.

He provides for the birds and all the creatures
Of course He loves His children and He is a
mighty teacher.
We learn patience, faith and hope while waiting
on our requests to be made by Him
Each produces strength that we didn't even
know we had and we are aware worrying is a
sin.
So let's put our faith to our actions in believing
on the ways God will provide,
Sometimes His answer is not right now, or He
will teach you how to live & survive.
Other times He answers right away before we
even have the very need,
We serve an amazing Dad who wants to show
His children that planting faith is planting a
seed.
Thank you God for all you have done and will
continue to do for us daily,
We take so much for granted and need to trust
you fully and not let worry be so heavy.
You take our burdens and place them in your
loving arms,
All you do for us in your own timing won't ever
cause us any harm.
You are one who listens to our silent prayers &
sees all of our eyes so teary
We are blessed to be able to go to God for
anything little or big & not become so weary.

Heaven's Full Moon

Oh what is the sky like from above at day and
night
with its twinkling stars glimmering oh what a
beautiful sight
To see the galaxy full of majestic colors of all
types,
How the moon must appear with the bright glow
with such might
No telescope could ever capture what is truly
there,
As all of Heaven looks down on earth how
unselfish of God with us to share
We only get to only dream of what space is
really made out to be
Such a magnificent Lord the creator of all in its
true wonder and glory
I don't know if man walked onto the moon
Only God alone knows what's up there and one
day we will also know quite soon
We see the moon only at night time in the dim of
the light,
But Heaven sees it all the time through both day
and night.
You see the moon reminds us that light is always
there

In this dark evil world the light of Christ can still
be found in our despair
The moon reminds me of someone letting their
light shine
In a place surrounded by sin and pain the flicker
gives way at just the right time.
The moon is important because without it there
would be total dark skies
The moon comes in many phases and never will
it wither & die.

Teddy Makes Days (Bear)able

The company gives ones a precious teddy bear
in memory of a baby girl or boy,
The bear is sweet temporary moments for us
Angel families to enjoy.
The little bear stands on its own, and doesn't
make a sound,
Just like the emptiness of the house when there
is no baby around
Our hearts & hands are empty without our
children here with us
Reaching out to get your own furry friend in
honor of your baby who has passed is a must,
We find it weird to some when we take our bear
to events
It gives us joy & peace when we find little
clothes to change it into, money well spent.
We have a little boy teddy & we call him our
precious Noah Bear,
We are very protective as if he were our own
baby, and we have great love & care.
Our bear will be with us in our family always &
forever
As the years go on and our family grows
stronger together.

So if you are seen hugging a small cuddly
friend,
Just know you aren't alone & we are holding
ours until the day comes to an end.
To the ones who hold a bear instead of a little
child
We see you & pray for your strength each day as
this journey of grief & pain is wild.
Our bear makes our days more bearable & our
dim holidays look very bright,
It's ok if you hold onto yours tightly through
your darkest nights.
We thank Barrett's Bears for our special fuzzy
little one,
I enjoy seeing others get their bears in memory
of their babies who have already gone.

God Heals Not Time

Living with grief is something I don't wish on
my worse enemy,
It entangles our hearts minds body and effects
our memory,
When one passes we fade away with them,
Losing ourselves sinking in an ocean of sorrow
we forget how to swim,
People say times heals and it gets better
For the ones grieving we just want to be all back
together
We change into people we have never seen
We grow angry, sad, bitter and sometimes very
mean,
We can't control when the grief will show it's
ugly head,
A song, smell, color, place can come our way
and we can be full of dread
We have moments where we just wish we were
with our loved ones
If we are saved by Jesus along with them then
are chances of seeing eachother isn't done.
Grief comes in many waves and various types
People can tell us how we should grieve but
there isn't an answer that is right.

We all grieve in different ways, some become so
busy they make the day go by so fast
Some can't get out of bed in the mornings and
wish that their bodies wouldn't last
Some want to hide in a dark room with not
hearing a sound
Some want to help the world and have a
community of people around
God gives us all of our emotions to be able to
grieve
Everyone has their own way of taking in the
precious memories
So I would say God heals all wounds and not
time alone
One day when we are with our loved ones we
will sing happy songs
If I didn't have God I don't know where I would
be in my journey of grief
I would probably shut down the world around
me.
I don't know what others do who don't have God
in their hearts and mind
They wouldn't be able to make it with peace
daily one moment at a time
So I encourage you to get right with the Lord
To see your loved ones again as you never know
when death knocks at your door.

Come As You Are

Jesus wants you to come to Him just as you are
Knowing He died on an old rugged cross for you
is the first start
Becoming a Christian is as a simple as ABC
Admitting, Believing & Confessing is the key
He paid the debt we could never pay for
ourselves so humbly
Once we accept Him into our hearts we will
have a glorious eternity.
Life isn't promised the next moment of day
Know Jesus before it's too late as He is the only
way!
No other religion has a living God like we do
The other gods are dead and can't do anything
for you.
I am thankful I serve a Savior so loving and so
true
My prayer is today that you accept Him as your
Lord & Savior too!

Never Alone

In our darkest hour or our brightest days
We can have confidence knowing that God will
go our way
He will not leave us in the wilderness, sinking or
crying at night
He is always with us guiding our hands by His
might
We think He leaves us by ourselves but that is
not true
He never leaves nor forsakes us in all we are and
in all that we do.
We may feel like we are the only one going
through pain
God feels our every sorrow, hurt and catches our
tears as they fall like the rain
We have a loving Father who cares for us so
deeply
One who holds our hand, walks beside us even
while we are beginning to get weak.
Thank you Lord that I am never alone
Your light shines through us and in us your love
is shown.

Is Christ In Your Life?

When people see you what do they see?
Do they see the love and light of Jesus in all His
glory?
Do they see a broken soul living for the world
and others?
Do they see a kind gentle soul like a loving
father or mother?
Do people wonder if you are living on the fence
Not able to chose between sin and righteousness.
We are said that we can be neither hot nor cold
each day
Living out the true word of God is the only right
way.
I pray Christ is living and dwelling on the inside
of you
Knowing that Jesus is your Savior & Lord gives
you peace too.
Make sure you are walking daily the Christian
walk
As well as talking to others with the Christian
talk
There are no grey areas when it comes to being
one with Him
Your light either shines very bright or it's hidden
by being dim.

Greatest of These Is Love

God created couples to be together
Knowing all the good and bad days they would
wether
He made man and woman to have and to hold
In sickness, health, pain and times of growing
old
Love is defined by so many ways and all various
types
Showing compassion, being selfless &
sacrificing their own likes,
It's more than just give and take in a marriage
It's sometime going 100% when the other can't
go on again
The movies make fairytales seem so simple
Marriage is work and the devil loves to destroy
it and our temples
Faith, Hope & Love is the 3 main components of
a happy family
Love is the greatest because God is love and we
are commanded to love with ease
Without love our families would fall apart and
be broken by a severed tie
Having the Love of the Father is how we can go
each day showing kindness in our life.

I am thankful to be able to give love to my
spouse
If God is the center of marriage than it surely
will be a blessed house.

We Made An Angel

It was supposed to look so different it was
supposed to look much better
We were to have a beautiful baby to take care of
and be together
You were perfect in every way 10 tiny toes &
little hands with 10 fingers so tiny
Too little for survival and for this cruel world
your little life was lived with ways so mighty
Having a baby is supposed to be filled with joy
and not pain
When you lose a baby your life becomes a flood
of grief with tear drops falling like rain.
We never got to see your beautiful eyes or your
sweet baby smile
The unknowing of the color they are makes our
hearts wonder everyday for a little while
You came too soon as my body was slowly
killing you
My little superhero came to save my life on a
hot summer day in June 2022.
We will forever remember our precious little boy
every moment of every day
One day when the time is right we will see our
boy again in the most glorious way.

Too Beautiful For Earth

To all the babies who were much too small
God sees the tears shed and loves them most of
all
He doesn't make mistakes and nothing is by a
chance
Our babies gone too soon are waiting on us to
come up with them to dance.
Our children are being well taken care of by the
hand of the Lord
The babies who were so innocent were protected
by the enemy's sword.
I like to imagine each birthday the babies
celebrate one another
They are playing with new friends and in the
field of flowers they pick together
Being a parent to an Angel is the worse kind of
sorrow
Knowing we will be reunited in Heaven we can
face the one who holds our tomorrow.

The Promise of a Rainbow

We know that rainbows come after the most
eventful storms
It shines through the clouds all 7 colors
profoundly like Heaven's open door
The rainbow represent's God promise to all
humanity
To never flood the earth again in it's whole as an
entirety
Satan has twisted the beautiful symbol and has
sadly made it his very own for his plan
He isn't creative and does things that's been done
before and so as Christians we must take a stand
The rainbow to some families is a beautiful
promise of a new life after loss
One after an Angel is called a rainbow baby &
the worry with another pregnancy comes at a
cost
The rainbow has beautiful distinct colors of 7
different shades
7 is completion since that's how many days it
took everything for God to create
When I see a rainbow in the sky I think about
children sliding happily down
For families all over rainbows represent joy, tiny
hands and new happiness in the town.

No matter what the day will hold we know a
rainbow is a promise from up above
That our world is protected because we have a
Father that is the definition of unconditional
love.

Numbered Days

How do you spend your day to day lives
Do you help others, or make others cry
Life is so short and is only here for a short little
while
We spend it growing families, chasing careers,
spending money or walking down the aisle.
Do people know your true identity
Or are you just getting by each day with just
existing
Are you helping when you are able to do much
more
Are you being a witness for Christ in the short
time with going door to door.
Do you pass the homeless people by without
stopping to lend a hand
Do you get involved with social matters that are
morally wrong do you even take a stand
Do you say you will be there for someone but
get so busy
Do you make time out of your schedule to offer
prayers for their eternity
Do you enjoy giving back when others are in
need of help
Do you prepare meals, fix things when they have
declining health

Do you sit back and say someone else will do
the things
One day it's too late to live a good life as the
time is up for Christ to get His kids
Good works are fine and all but will not get you
into the gates of eternity
Accepting Jesus as your Lord and Savior is how
you get to live forever victoriously.

Broken 2 Redeemed

It was a hot Summer night just like any other
one,
nothing was out of the ordinary I ate like I
always had done,
9pm I went to lay down not feeling well at all
Went to the bathroom and screamed for my
husband then frantically gave my mom a call.
Moments later rushing to be seen,
visiting hours were over and I was living a
horrible dream,
Only it wasn't a dream it was a nightmare so real
and so suddenly
They took me to the floor where babies were
being born safe and healthy,
The nurse checked his heartbeat one last time
very cautiously
No distress was there and it was going strong at
150
Moments later they tell me I was already at a 4
While my husband & mom waited in the next
room, the nurse called out the door
Wait, how could this be happening so soon
I was only 21 weeks with him not expecting this
kind of news of doom.
We had just seen him the week right before

His perfect little feet, hands, legs and arms
The lady said he wouldn't make it due to being
so tiny
His little lungs weren't formed yet and just had a
heart beating
21 weeks there was nothing at all they can do
If I was just a little further along we could have
had a place or two
Still believing in the power of prayer and God's
mighty healing hand
We thought maybe he wouldn't come that night
but their was a change of plans
I don't remember very much leading up to this
event
At 1:02am the most beautiful baby boy was born
and gone was my strength
The nurse had him all bundled in a tiny cloth
blanket
Confused as to why she was rocking him with
careful intent
She said he has a heartbeat do you want to hold
him
Those 30 minuets flew extra quickly with tear
filled eyes & our hopes fading dim
My husband held him the other half of the time
giving him his love & all
tiny in his huge hands his little waist just past his
wrists and he just bawled

Our precious little one with mommy's lips and
perfect little nose
Long little fingers and daddy's long toes
We didn't get to see the color of his little eyes
A heartbeat for just an hour and then at 2am our
hearts shattered and died
When he left us that morning Jesus brought him
into His glorious majesty
He was surrounded by passed loved ones who
are waiting for us with the King of Kings
Heaven got a new member that day up high in
the clouds
A little baby boy who was simply too beautiful
for this cruel earth and never made a sound
Our Noah was so precious & so very innocent
He is one child that Satan can never touch with a
single sin.
We miss him so much & look for signs of his
presence daily
God is our only source of strength, grace, love &
mercy
We will see our boy again one day soon when
we get to Heaven joyfully
We know he makes friends with all the angel
babies daily
we will forever love our beautiful boy our little
Noah Gray Talley.
We don't wish this grief and and pain on anyone
not even or enemies

If you have loss a baby know that you are never
alone there are parents on a daily basis
struggling
Losing a baby is the hardest heartache we have
ever had to go through everyday quietly
Knowing we will see him again gives us peace,
joy, comfort and one day our pain will come to
an end.
We had great hopes and dreams for our baby boy
God needed him more and wanted him to have a
perfect life of wonder to enjoy.
Please know you are not alone in your journey
of grief & suffering
As you sit sadly thinking of your babies gone
much too soon Jesus is right there with us & you
daily.

www.ingramcontent.com/pod-product-compliance
Lightning Source LLC
La Vergne TN
LVHW010933200726
843509LV00013B/2203